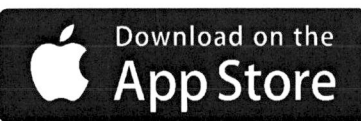

ISBN 978-1-330-96037-0
PIBN 10126672

1 MONTH OF
FREE
READING

at
www.ForgottenBooks.com

By purchasing this book you are eligible for one month membership to ForgottenBooks.com, giving you unlimited access to our entire collection of over 700,000 titles via our web site and mobile apps.

To claim your free month visit:

www.forgottenbooks.com/free126672

Similar Books Are Available from
www.forgottenbooks.com

THE BRITISH ACADEMY

THE ANNUAL SHAKESPEARE LECTURE
1915

Shakespeare and the Italian Renaissance

By

Sir Sidney Lee, D.Litt.
Fellow of the Academy

New York
Oxford University Press American Branch
35 West 32nd Street
London: Humphrey Milford

THE BRITISH ACADEMY

THE ANNUAL SHAKESPEARE LECTURE
1915

Shakespeare and the Italian Renaissance

By

Sir Sidney Lee, D. Litt.

Fellow of the Academy

New York
Oxford University Press American Branch
35 West 32nd Street
London: Humphrey Milford

SHAKESPEARE AND THE ITALIAN RENAISSANCE

By Sir SIDNEY LEE, D.Litt.

FELLOW OF THE ACADEMY

OUTLINE OF THE THEME

I. Italy's contribution to modern civilization.—The classical heritage.—The innovations of the Italian Renaissance.—The study of Plato and the Neo-Platonists.—The faith in physical beauty.—The new sense of colour.—The plea for intellectual enfranchisement.—The new scientific curiosity.—The federal bonds of European literature.

II. The significance of humanism.—Elizabethan debt to Italian stimulus.—Tudor travel in Italy.—Sir Philip Sidney in Venice. Italian visitors to England.—Giordano Bruno in London and Oxford. The study of Italian poetry and prose by Shakespeare's contemporaries. —Italian influence on Bacon's scientific speculation.

III. Shakespeare's humanism.—His intellectual receptivity.—His freedom from insularity combined with patriotic ardour.—The problem of his knowledge of Italian.—The Italian echoes in the moonlight scene in *The Merchant of Venice.*—The slenderness of Shakespeare's reference to Italian art.—His dramatic adaptations of Italian novels. His Italian scenes and characters.—*Romeo and Juliet, Twelfth Night,* `and *Othello.*—His *Sonnets* and the Italian conception of Platonism.— The traditional fascination of Italy in later English poetry.

I

LITERATURE, philosophy, science, law, and art are the five main currents of the tide of civilization. All the five trace much of their healthful flow in modern times within and without Europe to the impetus of Italian example—to the comprehensive energy in the fourteenth, fifteenth, and sixteenth centuries of Italy's imaginative, intellectual, and artistic accomplishment. Modern Italy's political history was until the middle of last century a record of gloom, a tale of cruel dismemberment; but her intellectual and artistic fortunes never ran higher than in the days of Shakespeare's youth. Literature and art gave a genuine meaning to the conception of Italian unity, even when the country was politically torn asunder by the strife of faction and by domestic or foreign tyrannies. A degenerate era of Italian culture opened at the close of the sixteenth century, but before that date Italy—by virtue of her art, poetry, and philosophy—had won unfading laurels for herself, and had helped many foreign brows to chaplets no less lasting. To change the metaphor, Italy may be fairly likened, in the fourteenth, fifteenth, and especially in the sixteenth century, to a copious fountain whence the sparkling waters of civilization spread in broad streams over modern Europe, and thence at later epochs, over a great part of the world. So honourable a tribute can be paid to no other country.

Italy set out on her modern career with advantages which she shared with no other part of Europe. Civilization in liberal measure illumined the land while mists of barbarism enveloped the rest of Europe.

The intellect of ancient Italy was largely fertilized by forces older and more lucent than those of her own breeding: by the thought and style of Greece. But the native land of Vergil and Catullus, of Cicero and Tacitus, insured herself near 2,000 years ago against a denial at any era of her literary genius or power. The country which harboured the Republic and Empire of Rome, the country which was the nursery of Roman law and the birthplace of Latin Christianity, claimed in the fifth century of our era a civilized and a civilizing tradition, which Attila and his Huns, with other scourges of kindred race, vowed to perdition in vain. The successes and failures of the Gothic warlords of the fifth century in their assaults on Italy graphically illustrate the virtual futility of relying on brute violence to annihilate the fruit of man's intellect and spirit.

The barbarian invaders of Italy effected a very incomplete conquest of the country, very incomplete when it is compared with their conquests elsewhere in Western Europe. In spite of the invasion and settlement of Teutons in the North, in spite of the later immigrations of Normans and Saracens in the South, the Latin race can still claim in the peninsula an ethnical predominance. On the lips of the people at large the old Latin language suffered in course of time transformation, re-formation. Yet the Latin tongue in select circles survived without radical decay and came to serve the greatest purposes of human intercourse, the purposes

of social organi   ducation, not in Italy alone, but
wherever goverr   on sure foundations by the barbarian conquerc   ph of the Latin language over the
perils of extinc   aced it in Europe of the fifth and
sixth centuries   tary testimony to the impotence of
brute matter ir   iconquerable mind.

Some 1,500   y proved herself the saviour of such
civilization as   i knew, and during some eleven suc-
ceeding centui   ged the proud function of protecting
the old elemen   n and reinforcing it with new elements.
The missiona   f civilizing Italy never suffered arrest
before the cl   eenth century. Yet the Teutonic influence bred in   ges sentiments and ideas which clouded
the mental a   tmosphere of all Europe and cast their
shadow on I   uld not exaggerate the darkness of the
Dark Ages :   ot disparage or ignore mediæval culture.
Much Latii   nd all Greek literature save Aristotle's
philosophical works were for the time lost. The Greek language
fell out of knowledge, and the lapse tended to impoverish the intellect. On the other hand, a substantial amount of Latin poetry
and prose was studied, and gave a cue to intellectual exertion.
Vergil and Ovid never lacked mediæval readers or commentators.
Aristotle in a Latin garb was reckoned the prophet of scholastic
philosophy. In Italy especially clear gleams of light broke the
mediæval sky. There was in the thirteenth century the poetry
of Dante, a brilliant radiance. None the less the teaching of the
old civilization endured in Italy a partial eclipse. The mediæval
Church enshrouded life and learning in a dim, mystical gloom of
which the ancient world knew little. The mind of man abandoned
itself to dreams and reveries.

The mediæval sentiment may be comprehensively defined as an
amalgam of dogma and asceticism. The mind and the body were
alike condemned to unprecedented restraints and austerities. The
monastic vows of obedience, poverty, and chastity well reflect the
mediæval aspiration. The piece of literature which best satisfied
the general temper had for its title ' the contempt of the world and
the miseries of the human condition.' Even Dante, who caught
many Pisgah-like glimpses of later enlightenment, saddened man
with his pictures of the Inferno, and he made his final goal peace
or quietism in all spheres of human endeavour. Dante's only hope
of realizing his ideal lay through universal recognition of a single
supreme authority, soaring above all calls of nationality as well

as individuality, a single supreme authority which should find em
bodiment in an omnipotent emperor.

In the fourteenth century there sprang from Italian soil a movement which had for its effect, if not for its first aim, the emanci
pation of human life and human aspiration from the fetters of
mediæval conceptions. The movement which we call the Renais
sance sprang up and matured on Italian soil, and confirmed Italy's
old title of saviour or champion of European civilization.

It was the gradual discovery by Italy of the true range of
classical Greek literature and philosophy which was the spring of
the intellectual and spiritual revival. That discovery was begun
in the fourteenth century, when Greek subjects of the falling
Byzantine Empire brought across the Adriatic manuscript memo-
rials of Greek intellectual culture, of which the West had lost
nearly all knowledge for some 1,000 years. Petrarch and
Boccaccio, the fathers of modern Italian literature, although they
were in no true sense Greek scholars, vaguely heralded the new
Greek revelation. But close study of Greek texts was needed
to bring home the significance of the new learning. It was not till
the overthrow of the Byzantine Empire by the Turks in the fifteenth century that the literary art of Athens was driven west-
ward in full flood, and the scope of Greek enlightenment was defi-
nitely acknowledged by Italy. It was then there first came into
the modern world the feeling for form, the frank delight in life,
the unrestricted employment of the reason. An ancient literature
and an ancient philosophy had come to light to prove that the
human intellect possessed capacities which were hitherto unim-
agined, and to convict of futility the dogmatic and ascetic ideals
of the Middle Ages.

Perhaps the Greek author whose influence on the new movement
was largest was Plato. Some dim knowledge of his theories is
visible in mediæval literature; but Aristotle in a Latin garb was the
only Greek philosopher who enjoyed any genuine allegiance in
Europe before the fifteenth century. On foundations, which the
Latinized Aristotle had laid, the Roman Church indeed built up its
intricate scheme of scholasticism. Direct study of the work of
Plato and of the Neo-Platonists, his late Greek disciples, was an
innovation of the Renaissance. At Florence, in the villa of the
Medici, the old Athenian Academy was revived in the fifteenth
century for the discussion of Plato's conception of life and love
and art. Under the banner of Florence the sway of mediævalism
received its first challenge.

At the outset the true issues of the strife were obscured. The Platonists of fifteenth-century Florence were slow to recognize the revolution which they were putting in train. Plato's predilection for abstractions and for allegory was not out of harmony with the intellectual tendencies of the Middle Ages, and mediæval processes of thought were very gradually abandoned by the Florentine academicians. The new literature and speculation abundantly illustrate the tenacity of the old spirit. The Florentine Platonists thought to reconcile the new enlightenment with the old scholasticism, and their jumbling of incompatible ideas drawn respectively from paganism and Christianity hindered for a generation a clear outlook. A wild incongruity infected Florentine art as well as Florentine speculation. Even Michael Angelo brought on canvas into the presence of the Madonna fauns disporting themselves in Dionysiac revels. Yet in time the Platonic light pierced the haze. At any rate the earth ceased to connote for the Italian Platonists gloom and misery; the human body was no longer a synonym for corruption; the reason grew impatient of servitude to any preconceived theory.

It was the idealization and worship of beauty that lit, in the groves of the Florentine academy, the flame which at length dispelled the mediæval vapour. The identification by the thinkers— first of Florence, then of other Italian cities, and afterwards of all the Western continent—of the highest good with beauty, the assumption that a true appreciation of beauty was the least disputable of virtues, went near shattering the dominant mediæval conceptions of the world and of humanity. The doctrine which found exponents through the length and breadth of Italy soon had its apostle in the papal curia itself. Cardinal Bembo summed up the new gospel by declaring that only when one said of the world that it is ' beautiful ' did one serve the cause of truth. ' Beautiful ' was, the cardinal argued, the only epithet which accurately described the heaven or the earth, the sea or the rivers, trees, gardens, or cities.

One of the practical fruits of the new Italian conception of beauty merits a special emphasis. Italian painting is one of the insistent facts in the history of the Renaissance. Italian painting is the first satisfying realization in the human economy of the significance of colour. The Italian painters of the Renaissance first interpreted life with any approach to perfection in terms of colour. The moving cause lay in Italy's new search in the creation for beauty. The Italian painters were fortunately placed. A relevant inspiration lay in the blue of the Italian sea and of the Italian sky, in the mingled hues of the native marble, in the gay plumage of the birds, in the immense variety of iridescent flowers, in the fruit of the vines, in the trees of the olive and the orange and the palm, and, last but not least, in the brilliant tints of Italian women's hair and complexion. Beauty of form was fully realized by the Greeks; but the Italian sense of colour was denied them. A full appreciation of colour in all the richness of its range is to be reckoned among the innovations of the Italian Renaissance. It is an original gift to the world of Titian and Tintoretto and other great painters of Italy to which poetry as well as art lay under obligation.

The new conception of beauty which challenged the old ideals of asceticism greatly stimulated the new conception of man's intellectual faculty which dealt a heavy although by no means a fatal blow at the mediæval principle of dogma. The creed of the Renaissance frankly acknowledged the earthly elements, the animal senses, in man's being. The fleshly instincts were often allowed freer play than before. Yet without pause did the missionaries of the Renaissance urge that man differed from all terrestrial creatures by virtue of his endowment of reason and that that endowment was capable of lifting him high above the animals, and of setting him ultimately on a level with the angels. The final purpose of reason harmonized in the creed of the Renaissance philosophy with the new faith in beauty. The mind of man was destined to discover and reveal the ultimate beauty and order which lay behind the outer shapes of matter.

Pico della Mirandola, a Renaissance philosopher, seems first to have invented for himself the proud title of ' interpreter of nature.' The title suggests the comprehensive potentiality which was attached to man's intellectual faculty. There were more avenues than one by which he might arrive at an interpretation of nature. A wide choice was offered him. Poetry, art, and philosophy, might each prove a pathway, and there was a fourth road which gave equal promise of the desired goal. The fourth approach lay through scientific inquiry. The intellectual restlessness of the Renaissance was impatient of specialization, and many Italian sons of the movement trod all the ways which seemed to incline in the right direction. Leonardo da Vinci is the most familiar type of the intellectual versatility of the era; he sought with almost equal enthusiasm to conquer the domains of science as well as of poetry and art.

Scientific curiosity issued from the new sense of beauty and the new plea for intellectual enfranchisement, in as compelling a flow as the artistic or literary achievement of the Renaissance. Nowhere in sixteenth-century Europe was scientific exertion more active or more fruitful than in Italy. The year that witnessed the birth of Shakespeare at Stratford-on-Avon witnessed the birth in Pisa of Galileo, the greatest Italian man of science in a line of succession which was already long and distinguished.

No reference however cursory to the scientific activity of the Renaissance would be complete without passing mention of its chief practical outcome in the era, the discovery of the New World. The first voyages across the Atlantic, which resulted in the momentous discovery of the Western hemisphere, were undertaken by way of testing a scientific theory or guess which was propounded in Italy in the early years of the Renaissance. The first two navigators who touched American shores—Columbus in the south and Cabot in the north—although they served foreign masters on their Atlantic explorations, were both natives of the great Italian seaport of Genoa. The intellectual stir, which came of the discovery of an old civilization (that of Greece) and put a new valuation on nature and man's intellectual capacity, was reinforced at no distant interval by the discovery of a new world which gave a new estimate of man's physical environment. The dark curtains which had hitherto restricted man's view of the physical world to a small corner of it were torn asunder, and the stimulating fact came to light that that which had hitherto been regarded by men as the whole sphere of physical life and nature was in reality a mere fragment of a mighty expanse, of the greater part of which there had been no previous knowledge. The intellectual revelation came first. The physical revelation followed. It was not a wholly accidental conjuncture of events. The new intellectual curiosity was first conspicuously justifying itself. Each revelation powerfully reacted on the other, and increased the fertility of Renaissance thought and action.

An English critic has written:

' Producers of great literature do not live in isolation, but catch light and heat from each other's thought. A people without intellectual commerce with other peoples has never done anything conspicuous in literature.'

The Greek influences of the Italian Renaissance adequately establish the pronouncement as far as Italy of that era is con-

cerned. What Greece did for Renaissance Italy, Renaissance Italy
did for contemporary Europe. The Italian influences of the
Renaissance moved in the sixteenth century the imagination of
her neighbours, France and Spain. Germany and England owed
great part of their literary and artistic aspiration in the sixteenth century to intellectual commerce with Italy. In England,
France, and Spain great heights of literary endeavour were in due
time scaled. There was no complete reciprocity with Italy in the
exchange of literary or artistic stimulus. The star of Italian
influence was in the ascendant throughout the epoch, and while
she shared her radiance with the other countries of Western Europe,
she received for a long time little compared with what she gave.
Yet Italy was not inattentive to contemporary advances of culture
outside her own boundaries in the sixteenth century, especially
in the way of scientific speculation. Ideas enjoyed a freedom of
intercourse which surmounted all the practical obstacles. In none
of the intellectual and artistic fields did nationality prove a bar to
communication. In the result Western Europe of the sixteenth
century formed something like a single federation of thought and
art, a fact which Bacon recognized when he left by will his name
and memory to foreign nations. Voltaire subsequently wrote to
an English friend: ' Ceux qui aiment les arts sont tous concitoyens.
Les honnêtes gens qui pensent ont à peu près les mêmes principes,
et ne composent qu'une seule et même république.' Voltaire's
vision was amply realized in the days when Shakespeare was setting
out on his mighty career.

II

The term ' humanist,' when it was first invented in Italy, merely
denoted a student of human or secular literature as distinguished
from sacred learning or theology. The first ' humanist ' was above
all things a classical scholar, and ' humanism ' was little more than
a synonym for classical scholarship. But classical study, as we
have seen, sharpened and widened all human faculty, and the word
humanist ' may be justly extended to apply to all who in the
sixteenth century were inspired by the new faith in beauty and
reason, to all who sought to realize the new exalted hopes of human
progress.

England was somewhat slow to enlist in this mighty march of
mind. The culture of the Renaissance blossomed late in the British
isle, far later than in Italy, or indeed in France. Nor did the English soil prove equal to fostering the humanist development in all

the fields of endeavour which the new spirit fructified in Italy. No original painting, no original music, were cradled in Tudor England. There the Renaissance sought distinctive expression in literature and poetry alone. Nor was it till the last years of the sixteenth century that the literature or the poetry of Tudor England acquired true distinction. But although her pace was sluggish through the earlier decades, England was steadily garnering, as they passed, foreign stimulus, chiefly Italian stimulus. Not all the foreign impetus was the exclusive gift of Italy. On the one hand, Englishmen came to study the classics for themselves, and, on the other, they soon had at their disposal the Renaissance literature of France. Yet French literature of the sixteenth century was itself to a large degree fruit of the Italian tree. Much of the spirited teaching which France offered her neighbour had been learnt in Italian schools. The French liberality of suggestion helped to reinforce in literary England Italian influence. But the foreign influences, whencesoever they came, worked efficiently They braced the native genius to triumphant exertion which left Elizabethan literature a match for the world.

Humanism in England may be dated from the visit of the three Oxford scholars, Linacre, Grocyn, and Colet, to Florence and other cities of Italy at the end of the fifteenth century. Colet's friend, Sir Thomas More, showed at the opening of the following century a sensitiveness to the new enlightenment which entitles him to be regarded as its earliest English apostle. His *Utopia* ranks with the richest fruits of the new Renaissance study of Plato; but it should be borne in mind that More's first publication was a translation into English of a pregnant biography of Pico della Mirandola, a Florentine pioneer of that interpretation of Platonic philosophy which was re-forming the human intellect. Sir Thomas More justly called Pico 'a great lord of Italy and an excellent cunning man in all sciences.'

Englishmen acquired early that habit of Italian travel which they have not yet lost. English visitors to the great Italian cities always made careful report at home of the new revelations of Italian thought. In the middle years of the century one Sir Edward Hoby visited Venice, then in all her splendour, as well as Padua and Mantua, Ferrara, Siena, and Rome. It was Hoby who rendered into English the very textbook of the Renaissance culture of Italy, *Il Cortegiano* ('The Courtier') by Baldassare Castiglione. That volume pictured in minutest detail the scholar and the gentleman as he had been fashioned by the new ideals, and the theme was rounded off by a rapturous oration assigned to Cardinal Bembo on the new conceptions of beauty and of love.

English travellers in sixteenth-century Italy, despite political and religious controversy, were hospitably entertained. They were impressed not merely by the country's intellectual and artistic triumphs, but by the refined amenities of her social life. Academies on the Florentine model had made the literary club for conversation and discussion a prominent feature of civic organization. Art had touched the domestic furniture and equipment, and had brought into use devices and implements which were barely known in England. Many an English visitor to Italy was surprised to find forks habitually taking the place of fingers. Throughout Shakespeare's lifetime Englishmen explored Italy in numbers which increased year by year. There were protests from time to time on grounds of morality or religion. Rome, it was urged, was no fit place of pilgrimage for an English Protestant. The practical ethics of the Italian people were held to falsify conspicuously the lofty standards of their ideal philosophy. Some stern English moralists judged that the opportunity of vicious indulgence, the notorious enchantments of Italian Circes, were the main incentives to Italian travel. Englishmen in Italy were reckoned indeed by some to better the Italian instruction in sin, so that men occasionally spoke of an Italianate Englishman as a devil incarnate. The Italian Renaissance, despite its high ideals and brilliant accomplishments, had a dark side which insular prejudice or intolerance was not likely to underestimate. Yet it was a negligible minority of Englishmen in Italy who suffered serious moral or religious deterioration. The most efficient leaders of public opinion never ceased to preach the value of travel as a necessary part of a good education, and it was to foreign Italian cities, with their memorable antiquities, libraries, colleges, theatres, and academies, that the young Englishmen were chiefly advised to bend their steps. If they were confronted by temptation there was benefit in the discipline of resistance. 'Homekeeping youth have ever homely wits,' wrote Shakespeare. A perfect man, he added, was one who was tried and tutored in the world outside his native country. The dramatist laughingly detected in the travelled Englishman no worse failing than a predilection for outlandish manners and dress which offended insular taste. When it was said of an Elizabethan that he 'had swum in a gondola,' the intention was to pay him a compliment on his polished deportment—on his urbanity, a trait which was first identified with Italian cities.

Sir Philip Sidney was perhaps more sensitive to the varied manifestations of the spirit of the age than any contemporary, and in his short life he illustrated by his own activities as graphically as any Englishman the versatility of the new forces of culture. His visit in youth to the home of the Renaissance, to Italy—while all the artistic, literary, and scientific impulses of the era were in full glow—attests the stimulating purpose which Italian travel commonly served. In Italy Sidney learned sonnetteering of the school of Petrarch. The pastoral romanticism which the Neapolitan Sanazzaro had brought to birth in his Italian *Arcadia* impelled Sidney to furnish his fellow countrymen with an English Arcadia—a region which it would rather puzzle serious geographers to find on the map. Sanazzaro first applied the geographical Greek name of Arcadia to an imaginary realm of pastoral simplicity, where love-making was the sole concern of life. It was largely, too, under the sway of Italian criticism that Sidney sought in his *Apology for Poetry* to shame the earth-creeping mind ' into lifting itself up to look into the sky of poetry.' But Sidney's craving for knowledge under Italian skies passed beyond these bounds. He did not limit his observation to literature in his Italian tour. At Venice, where he remained longest, he devoted a great part of his time to astronomy and music, a science and an art which absorbed immense Italian energy despite other distraction. Furthermore Sidney enjoys the rare distinction among Elizabethans of coming into personal contact with the two great Italian painters, Tintoretto and Paolo Veronese. With those men the pictorial art of Venice came near perfection. Each offered to paint Sidney's portrait, and he was embarrassed by the choice. Whether he was wise in selecting Paolo Veronese I leave to the judgment of those who know more of art than I do. The portrait was completed by Veronese, and all lament that it is not known to survive.

Yet it was not essential for an Englishman of Shakespeare's era to visit Italy in order to keep in touch with her literary activities or philosophic progress. There were from time to time Italian visitors to England, who were capable of giving to Englishmen in their own country instruction in the new Italian culture by word of mouth. An Italian professor of law, Alberico Gentili, an Italian jurist of the highest reputation in his own country, taught Roman law for many years at Oxford, and gave a new impulse to its study in England. But the most notable of the Italian visitors to this country while Shakespeare was a youth was the Platonic philosopher, Giordano Bruno, whom Coleridge classes with Dante and Ariosto as one of the three most characteristic Italians of all time. Bruno was a philosopher and a scientific inquirer of the type dear to the Renaissance. He sought out the beauty of the world and discovered it in a light flowing from heaven. He defended the new Copernican system of astronomy which makes the earth a satellite of the sun. In a mystical allegory, *Spaccio de la Bestia Trionfante*, he foretold how the elements of man's lower nature were to vanish, and their places to be filled by truth, prudence, and wisdom—wisdom whose daughter is law. In his *Gli Eroici Furori* Bruno distinguished two kinds of enthusiasm, one which bred blind and unreasoning fanaticism, and the other which bred that love of truth and justice which turns some men into prophets and teachers and other men into creative artists. This noble prophet of enlightenment, who delivered his message to the chief universities of Europe in turn, arrived in England in 1583 and stayed here nearly two years. A warm welcome was accorded him by Sir Philip Sidney and his friends, and in many a debate on mighty themes did he engage them under their own roofs. Not all England was prepared to accept his ethereal teaching. He obtained permission of the Vice-Chancellor of Oxford to lecture in that University, and announced himself as ' the awakener of sleeping souls ' ('dormitantium animarum excubitor'), but his audience disappointed him by their somnolence. He consoled himself by bitterly describing Oxford as ' una costellazione di pedantesca ostinatissima ignoranza e presunzione mista con una rustica inciviltà, che farebbe prevaricar la pazienza di Giobbe.' Nor could he refrain from complaints of the bad manners of the English people, their uncouth language, and their detestable climate. Yet whatever the discouragements of academic Oxford and the discomforts of his English sojourn, Bruno, while he lived in stimulating converse with men of letters in London, wrote or planned the philosophic and scientific books on which his fame mainly rests. The dedication of two of these works—*Spaccio de la Bestia Trionfante* and *Gli Eroici Furori*—to Sir Philip Sidney is a tribute to a fellow countryman in which we may all take pride. Elizabethan England at large may hardly have been ready for Bruno's gospel; but she at any rate placed no restriction on his freedom of thought. He enjoyed here, in his own phrase, an inestimable ' libertas philosophandi.' In his own country the forces of dogma had been checked but not crushed, and scientific originality was a chief abhorrence of the conservative temper. Bruno's boldness of utterance finally exposed him to the cruel reproof of the Inquisition, that blind protector of the ancient creeds. In the last year of the sixteenth century Bruno was burnt at the stake in Rome. He cheerfully sacrificed life in the cause of knowledge. It is some satisfaction to know that since 1889 there has stood a statue of this Italian guest and friend of Sir Philip Sidney in Rome itself, on the very spot—the Campo di Fiore—where the faggots once blazed about his helpless frame.

But beyond the visit of Englishmen to Italy or of Italians to England, there lay a far vaster opportunity of acquiring in England a knowledge of Italian poetry and philosophy. At the moment that Shakespeare was absorbed in the great work of his life, the domestic facilities may be gauged by the issue in English renderings of the two most imposing manifestations of the Italian poetic genius of the era. The most characteristic verse of sixteenth-century Italy was the epic poetry of Ariosto and Tasso. Each poet's temperament illustrates to perfection a salient phase of the Italian genius of the Renaissance, and together they present its whole range. Both tell a story with spirit; both are masters of verbal melody; both have the painter's eye for imagery. But the boundless energy and kindly irony of Ariosto are replaced in Tasso by romantic pathos and deep-toned lyric harmony. To both their idiosyncrasies Elizabethan translators were found capable of doing justice. The greatest English epic of the period, Spenser's *Faerie Queene*, owes much to the inspiration of these Italian poets. Spenser avowedly set himself to ' overgo ' or excel Ariosto, and an admission of his success is quite consistent with a liberal appreciation of the many stirring episodes and fancies which he borrowed from Ariosto's pages. The most exquisite canto which Spenser penned, the sixth of the second book, is touched in nearly every line by Tasso's sensuous enchantment.

Time will not permit of more than a hint of the Italian influences which worked immediately on Elizabethan lyric or sonnet. ' The sweet Tuscan,' as Petrarch was called by Elizabethan poets, was the confessed master of the Elizabethan sonnet. Spenser was reckoned by Elizabethan critics so expert a pupil that he was often called ' the English Petrarch.' Spenser's lyric fancy was steeped moreover in the philosophy of the Florentine Platonists, while Tasso was one of a hundred other Italian poets who trained the lyric inspiration of Shakespeare's contemporaries. Samuel Daniel's lyric charm is not in question. Yet it is doubtful if without the tuition of Tasso and some other foreign masters (French as well as Italian), he would have won his high place in our literature. Here are some beautiful lines from his pen:

> Let's love, the sun doth set and rise again;
> But when as our short light
> Comes once to set, it makes eternal night.

Although Daniel gave no hint that he owed the verse to any out-side suggestion, he was translating, as literally as the two languages admitted, the pensive words of Tasso:

> Amiam, che 'l Sol si muove, e poi rinasce.
> A noi sua breve luce
> S' asconde, e 'l sonno eterna notte adduce.

If we pass to prose, especially to prose on speculative topics, we find the processes of assimilation, translation, or adaptation from the Italian at work with equal vigour. When Bacon declares his hostility to Aristotle, and insists on the superiority of experi-ment and induction over deduction or ratiocination untested by direct observation, he admits indebtedness to a philosopher who lately lived and wrote in the extreme south of Italy, to Telesio of Cosenza. Bacon curiously calls Telesio an Italian ' novelist,' meaning an Italian innovator of scientific method. When Bacon dubbed himself an ' interpreter of nature,' he borrowed the title from the Florentine Platonist, Pico della Mirandola. As in poetry, so in science, Italian hints often blossomed in English minds into imagination or thought of unexpected power and scope. William Harvey, the discoverer of the circulation of the blood, graduated in 1602 in the medical school of Padua University, after attending the lectures of the Italian professor who was the greatest anato-mist of his day. The help of his great Italian teacher is not to be gainsaid. Yet Harvey passed far beyond the range of his Italian study when he gave medical and physiological knowledge a new certitude.

III

I claim Shakespeare as the greatest of humanists in the broad sense which the term justly bears in the history of the Italian Renaissance. I believe that in Shakespeare the spirit of humanism worked to supreme effect. Were I casting a discourse on humanism in the mould of a sermon and prefacing it with texts, I doubt if

I could do better than choose two passages from Shakespeare. There are two familiar passages in the play of *Hamlet* each of which expresses with admirable point one or other of the two most significant phases of the Renaissance—the cry for intellectual enfranchisement on the one hand and the enthusiasm for man's physical and mental endowments on the other. The first passage runs:

> Sure He that made us with such large discourse,
> Looking before and after, gave us not
> The capability and god-like reason,
> To fust in us unused.

The second runs:

'What a piece of work is a man! how noble in reason! how infinite in faculty! in form and moving how express and admirable! in action how like an angel! in apprehension how like a god! the beauty of the world! the paragon of animals!'

It would be easy to match the first passage in the writings of Giordano Bruno. The second passage seems to echo the raptures of Pico della Mirandola. Elsewhere Shakespeare makes himself responsible for yet another opinion which precisely reflected the intellectual tendency of the era. From his pen came the words 'Modest doubt is called the beacon of the wise.' Many times too does the dramatist reinforce Hamlet's salutation of the potential beauty of human nature by enthusiastic greetings of the beauties of physical nature in which the new Italian sense of colour seems to be craving an original utterance. When Shakespeare wrote,

> Full many a glorious morning have I seen
> Flatter the mountain tops with sovereign eye,
> Kissing with golden face the meadows green,
> Gilding pale streams with heavenly alchemy,

or when he hailed

> daffodils,
> That come before the swallow dares, and take [i.e. bewitch]
> The winds of March with beauty,

he testified to the same impulse which moved Cardinal Bembo, a generation before, to say that beauty is the essential attribute of the heavens and the earth, of rivers and gardens. Shakespeare's definition of man as ' the *beauty* of the world,' and the power which he detects in the daffodils of infatuating with their ' beauty ' the March winds, powerfully accentuate the Renaissance apostle's teaching. Every reader of Shakespeare will be able to add to these quotations, which interpret with all Shakespeare's gift of language paramount principles of the Italian Renaissance.

Intellectual receptivity, assimilative capacity, is an invariable mark of poetic genius. The popular apophthegm that the poet is born and not made needs much qualification before it can be credited with truth. The originality of genius is no mere spontaneous emanation or exhalation of the poet's mind. It is rather the magical power of absorbing very rapidly, even instantaneously, pre-existing thought and fancy, and of delivering them to the world again in a new and arresting shape or expression. Shakespeare's pre-eminence resides in his catholic sensitiveness to external impressions, whether they came from reading or from observation, and in his power of transmuting them in the crucible of his mind into something richer and rarer than they were before. All modes of thought and style wrought thus upon him. Among the many foreign influences to which he proved susceptible, I believe the teaching of the Renaissance looms as large as any in a just estimate of the sources of his achievement.

The needful recognition of the foreign element in the constitution of Shakespeare's achievement is quite compatible with the fullest acknowledgement of his patriotic sentiment which is clearly unassailable. While he must be absolved of all taint of insularity he cannot be suspected of cosmopolitanism in its undesirable significance. The bracing air of toleration fed his spirit; but that virtuous sustenance never impaired his love of his own country or his confident faith in her destiny. It was he who apostrophized his country and countrymen in his own magnificent diction as:

> This happy breed of men, this little world;
> This precious stone set in the silver sea,
> Which serves it in the office of a wall,
> Or as a moat defensive to a house
> Against the envy of less happier lands:
> This blessed plot, this earth, this realm, this England.

At the same time Shakespeare, with almost equal fervour, depre-
cates the shortness of vision which ignores the patriotism of other
countries, and refuses all fellow-feeling with them:

> Hath Britain all the sun that shines?   Day, night,
> Are they not but in Britain? . . . Prithee think
> There's livers out of Britain.

Shakespeare is at once the noblest expositor of patriotism, and the
most resolute contemner of insularity.

No one who has closely studied Shakespeare's writings can har-
bour any doubt of the breadth of his reading, or can view with
other than impatience the persistent fallacy, which Milton rashly
stamped with his authority, when he wrote of Shakespeare as
'fancy's child warbling his native woodnotes wild.'   The extent
to which Shakespeare studied Italian literature in the original
admits of discussion.   He quotes in Italian a proverbial compliment on the beauties of Venice in his earliest play, *Love's Labour's
Lost:*

> Venetia, Venetia,
> Chi non ti vede, non ti pretia.

Hamlet, when he talks to Ophelia of ' the players' ' play, remarks
that ' the story is extant, and written in very choice Italian.'
There is clear evidence too in the history of the composition of
Othello that the dramatist had access to at least one tale which
had never worn any but an Italian garb.   But the range of his
linguistic power does not matter very much.   He was in any case
far better versed in English than in any other tongue.   A large
part of Italian poetry and prose of the Renaissance was accessible
to him in English translation.   As students of Spenser know,
the fundamental ideas of the Renaissance and many literary
processes of the Renaissance—the Platonic interpretation of life
and the world, the decorative usage of classical mythology—were
already woven into the web of Elizabethan writing when Shakespeare was serving his apprenticeship to his art.   There were
many keys to open the gates of knowledge to a man of his alert
intuition.

To a large extent the Italian affinities of Shakespeare's work
were in all probability a vicarious endowment, but they were none
the less effective on that account.   The Elizabethan atmosphere

was so charged with Italian thought and fancy, that no sensitive poetic genius, even if Italian books were wholly sealed for him, could well escape an ample draught of inspiration.   In the familiar scene in *The Merchant of Venice*, where Lorenzo talks through the moon-lit night with Jessica in the gardens of Portia's villa, one hears throughout the dominant notes of the Italian Renaissance in all their sweetness.   The setting of the scene catches completely the Italian spirit.   The mythological reminiscences, the praise of music, the neo-Platonic and pseudo-scientific theory of the spheres, are all Italian or Greco-Italian echoes.

When Lorenzo points out to Jessica the floor of heaven, and tells her

> There's not the smallest orb which thou behold'st
> But in his motion like an angel sings,
> Still quiring to the young-eyed cherubins:

the scholarly reader may be forgiven for recalling the mystical speculation of a famous South Italian contemporary, Tommaso Campanella, poet and man of science, who out of a Platonic fancy elaborated a beatific vision of spirit-inhabitants of the stars, communicating thought to one another in words of light.   But I think we should be content to ascribe this and other surprising likenesses of thought and fancy between Shakespeare's poetry and Italian Renaissance speculation to agencies other than immediate recourse to Italian texts.

Shakespeare's specific references to Italian art are rare.   They do scant justice to the scope of the Italian triumphs in the realms of painting or of sculpture.   Yet Shakespeare on occasion makes vague reference to art at large which supplements the story of his intuitive relations with the doctrines of the Italian Renaissance. Once, and once only, Shakespeare paid an enthusiastic tribute to the life-like excellence of Italian sculpture.   But his praises seem to lack the precision which betokens first-hand knowledge.   In *The Winter's Tale* (v. ii. 93-9), the supposed statue of Hermione is described as ' a piece many years in doing and now newly performed by that rare Italian master, Julio Romano, who, had he himself eternity and could put breath into his work, would beguile Nature of her custom, so perfectly he is her ape.'   The speaker finally asserts that Romano ' so near to Hermione hath done Hermione, that they say one would speak to her and stand in hope of answer.'   Shakespeare's ' rare Italian master ' was an eminent pupil of Raphael. Vasari, the sixteenth-century biographer of Italian artists, cites an epitaph which imputes to him skill as a sculptor, no less than as a painter; but it is by his pictures alone that Romano is now known, and Shakespeare's panegyric cannot be literally corroborated. Nowhere else does the dramatist make a like categorical reference to an Italian artist of the Renaissance. More than once elsewhere, however, he grows almost ecstatic over the living illusion of great portraiture. He fails to associate the perfect art directly with Italy. Of the portrait of Timon of Athens by a painter who is nominally an Athenian, a critic who is also presented as an Athenian, exclaims (*Timon*, I. i. 40-1) ·

> It tutors Nature: artificial strife
> Lives in these touches, livelier than life.[1]

Whatever the limitations of Shakespeare's personal acquaintance with the artistic fruits of sixteenth-century Italy, he clearly assimilated a popular philosophic axiom of Italian criticism which represented the great sculptor or painter as a rival of creative Nature, and Nature herself as cherisher of a fear that the artist by improving on her handiwork might discredit her. Bembo, the Cardinal of the Renaissance, invested the theory with extravagance when he wrote on Raphael's tomb:

> Hic ille est Raphael, metuit quo sospite vinci
> Rerum magna parens, et moriente, mori.

(Here lies the famous Raphael, in whose life-time great mother Nature feared to be outdone, and at whose death feared to die.)

It is curious to note that the identical conceit was chosen to decorate Shakespeare's own epitaph in Stratford-on-Avon Church. The elegist, when he wrote of—

> Shakespeare, with whom
> Quick nature died,

placed the dramatist in that category of creative artists, to which Bembo had assigned Raphael. Shakespeare's poetic art was thus

---

[1] Cf. *Venus and Adonis* (289-92):
Look when a painter would surpass the life,
In limning out a well proportion'd steed,
His art with nature's workmanship at strife,
As if the dead the living should exceed.

identified by his own countrymen with the same conception of creative genius as that called into being by the pictorial art of the Italian Renaissance.

I have spoken of some ancillary glories of Shakespeare's dramatic poetry, and of the exalted conception of his artistic powers, which justly identified him with the sons of the Italian Renaissance. When we descend to the more material foundations of his work, the problem enters a somewhat different .phase. It is familiar knowledge that Shakespeare hewed many of his plays out of Italian stories. The most superficial studies of his plots show him to be beyond doubt a close student of a very distinctive species of literature which is peculiarly characteristic of Renaissance Italy. Boccaccio, of Florence, the herald of the new Italian movement in many of its directions, may be reckoned to have rendered his most conspicuous service to the amenities of civilization by his creation of the art of the short story. In musical language .which eliminated once and for all the crudities of the old Tuscan dialect, Boccaccio pictured, with a softly glowing serenity, experiences of love and life of which he had read or heard or seen. He treats human nature with a frankness which often shocks the prudish. He is .prone to dwell with a cheerful irony on the infidelities of husbands and wives. Yet he is a master of pathos as well as of gaiety, and blends varied ingredients harmoniously. Boccaccio the novelist founded in Italy a long-lived school, and though none of his scholars equalled his own powers, many who were especially active in the sixteenth century, caught some touch of his vivacity. Bandello, a Lombard, who was a bishop in the south of France at the time of Shakespeare's birth, turned into lively fiction of Boccaccio's type episodes in the social life of his day. Although he lacked his master's gift of style Bandello excelled Boccaccio in lubricity. A third sixteenth-century Italian novelist, Giraldi Cinthio, of the cultured city of Ferrara, also enjoyed a wide reputation in his day. In his methods, merits, and demerits he may be linked with Bandello. The Italian novel, indeed, engaged almost as much energy in Renaissance Italy as the drama subsequently engaged in Elizabethan or Jacobean England. It found readers, not in Italy alone, but, either in the original or in translation, in all countries of Western Europe. Imitations as well as translations soon abounded in France, Spain, and ultimately in England.

The Italian novel rendered the English drama the practical service of supplying it with a treasury of plots, and Shakespeare, like all the fellow dramatists of his time, welcomed with enthusiasm such practical help. Most but not all the Italian stories which he employed were ready to his hand in his own language or in French. His indebtedness to Italy is not, however, greatly reduced thereby. The English and French renderings at his command, though differing among themselves in efficiency, were usually literal. Their temper was little changed. In whatever shape Shakespeare gained access to them, the main stories of *All's Well that Ends Well* and *Cymbeline*, of which Helena and Imogen are the respective heroines, remain the ripe fruit of Boccaccio's invention. Bandello is the parent of the leading episodes of *Romeo and Juliet* and *Much Ado About Nothing*. Cinthio was the first to tell the tragic adventure of Isabella in *Measure for Measure* and the tragic trials of Othello and Desdemona. Even where Shakespeare seeks his plot in romances of English authorship, as in *As You Like It* and *The Winter's Tale*, the Italian influence is not wholly absent; for the English novelists commonly marched along the Italian road: they rarely travelled far from it.

The Italian fable, it goes without saying, formed as a rule the mere basis of Shakespeare's dramatic structure. Having studied the Italian tale and examined its dramatic possibilities, Shakespeare altered and transmuted it with the utmost freedom as his dramatic spirit moved him. It is by his changes rather than by his literal transferences that the greatness of his faculty, the breadth of his intuitive grasp of human passion and sentiment, may best be gauged.

Yet the scenes of his chief comedies and of many tragedies rarely leave Italy. The episodes are assigned to Venice or Verona, to Milan or Mantua, to Florence or Padua. He rarely takes the names of his characters from the Italian novels of his immediate study. He rechristens his *dramatis personae*, but the new designations are no less Italian than the old. It is curious to observe that, when in *As You Like It* Shakespeare is dramatizing a piece of English fiction by his fellow countryman, Thomas Lodge, he rejects Lodge's amorphous name of Rosader for his hero and substitutes a name so rooted in the traditions of Italian literature as Orlando. I think it provable that Shakespeare's Orlando, the hero of *As You Like It*, was deliberately christened after the Orlando of Ariosto's great Italian epic. Shakespeare's Italian nomenclature may not always suggest quite so much as that; but it invariably proclaims him the pupil of an Italian school, paying homage to his masters.

At times Shakespeare's choice of Italian plot sets his work in the full tide of the Italian literary stream. The story of Romeo and Juliet, which Bandello first told to Europe, was made familiar to Italy by earlier pens. The tale, which has a right to be reckoned a national legend of Italy, was the theme of Shakespeare's earliest venture in tragedy of the great romantic kind. In his dramatic treatment of it, he gave indubitable promise of his glorious fertility and power. Manifold are the original touches of poetry, insight, and humour in Shakespeare's version of the Italian novel. Yet who can deny the Italian glow which lives in Shakespeare's radiant picture of youthful love?

The play of *Twelfth Night* is cast in a very different mould from that of *Romeo and Juliet*. Everybody knows the main plot, how a girl is disguised as a page; and how, while her master moves her love, she is sent by him to plead his suit with a proud beauty, who on her part is fascinated by the supposed boy. The fable is a fantasy of which all the elements are dyed in Italian colours. Bandello, although he gave the story its European vogue, was, as in the case of *Romeo and Juliet*, but one of its Italian narrators. No English alchemy could free the sensitive and intricate amours of their Italian note. Shakespeare's play, in spite of his manipulation of the Italian plot and his fusion with it of much original comic episode, echoes the strains which Boccaccio's youths and maidens voiced in the garden overlooking Florence at the dawn of the Italian Renaissance. What atmosphere save that of sensuous Florence does Duke Orsino breathe when in the first speech of the play he makes languorous appeal to the musicians:

> That strain again! it had a dying fall:
> O, it came o'er my ear like the sweet sound
> That breathes upon a bank of violets,
> Stealing and giving odour.

Shakespeare's tragedy of *Othello*, the best constructed of all his tragic dramas, presents life in its sternest aspect and passion in its fiercest guise. Yet it is based as directly as *Romeo and Juliet* and *Twelfth Night* on Italian foundations, and, unlike the other Italian stories whence Shakespeare drew his plots, the fable of *Othello* is not known to have circulated out of Italy, or rather out of the Italian language, before Shakespeare handled it. The author of the story of Shakespeare's tragedy of *Othello* is the sixteenth-century novelist, Cinthio of Ferrara. Some of his tales had been rendered into French, and at least one into English. Before Shakespeare wrote *Othello* he had himself made a first draft on Cinthio's store of fiction. The plot of *Measure for Measure* was of Cinthio's devising; but that painful Italian story was ready to Shakespeare's hand in an English version. Not so the little novel of the Moor of Venice. In the Italian alone was that tragic history to be studied. In adapting the incidents to his purpose, Shakespeare here if anywhere exerted all his powers. With magical subtlety he invests the character of Othello with passionate intensity, of which the Italian novelist knew little. Iago is transformed by the English dramatist from the conventional Italian criminal of Cinthio's page into the profoundest of all portraits of hypocrisy and intellectual villany. At every point Shakespeare has lifted the theme high above the melodramatic level on which the Italian had left it. New subsidiary characters are added. The catastrophe is wholly reconstructed. The master spirit is everywhere at work with magnificent energy. Yet Cinthio's guidance is not to be disparaged. His story holds the sparks which Shakespeare's genius fanned into brilliant flame.

Finally, let me supplement what I have already said of the tinges of Platonic philosophy, which the Italian Renaissance conveyed to Shakespeare's pages, by a concluding reference to his *Sonnets*. It would be irrelevant to my present purpose to mention, let alone discuss, any of the difficult problems which attach to these poems. At the moment I merely cite them as consummating evidence of the genuine strength of Shakespeare's affinities with Italian Platonism. Responsive as he proves himself elsewhere to varied influences of the Renaissance, I believe that the *Sonnets* prove even more convincingly than any other of his writings how deeply he had drunk of the spring of Italian philosophy. All the sonnetteers of Europe, from their father Petrarch downwards, enlisted under Plato's banner and preached the ideality of beauty, isolating it from its physical embodiment. As Platonic or Neo-Platonic study widened in Italy, much lyric poetry there and elsewhere assimilated in greater and greater degree the technicalities of Plato's or the Neo-Platonists' mystical conception. Michael Angelo, one of the noblest Italian champions of the Renaissance, wrote sonnets, in which the loveliness of earthly things is invariably held to reflect an ethereal light from heaven. Shakespeare immersed himself as a sonnetteer in even deeper metaphysical subtleties. Constantly he credits the beauty of the friend whom he celebrates with the qualities of a ' shadow '—the English rendering of the technical

Latin word *umbra* which Giordano Bruno and other Italian Platonists applied to the mundane reflection of their idea or ideal of perfection—an idea or ideal which lay outside the material world. The beauty of Shakespeare's friend is (he tells us) a ' shadow ' of the true ' substance ' of perfect beauty; the substance is not visible to mortal eye, only the shadow is seen on earth. Shakespeare goes even a step further in his metaphysical theorizing in the *Sonnets*. Beauty in its unearthly perfection he identifies with truth, again an entity which is independent of matter and indeed of time. Constantly Shakespeare links truth and beauty together, as of the same ethereal significance and quality. The meaning of his phraseology is, as is common in such debate, often obscure. But there is no reason to doubt that one of the doctrines by which he stood when he penned his sonnets was an anticipation of Keats's mystical creed:

> Beauty is truth, truth beauty; that is all
> Ye know on earth, and all ye need to know.

It was by way of Italy that such doctrine reached Shakespeare in England.

Shakespeare's work is a vast continent, and I this afternoon am only endeavouring within the limits of my power and my hour to explore a single stretch of the territory. There are many, and my sympathies are with them, who detect in Shakespeare's humour his greatest gift. That endowment and his manner of exercising it owe nothing to Italy. Italian humour was pitched in another key. Nor can Italy claim any influence on his masterly reform of the methods of drama, and on his triumphant broadening of its bases. Italian drama of the sixteenth century was too closely wedded to the classical canons to touch at many points a dramatic ambition, which sought to realize in the theatre the highest ideals of romance, and to set adrift theatrical conventions in manifest conflict with the representation of sentient life. The brisk dialogue of Shakespearean comedy and the portrayal there of some veteran types of eccentricity may occasionally echo an Italian note. But the profundities of Shakespearean tragedy lay beyond the Italian range. The Italian Renaissance was but one of the forces which went to the making of Shakespeare's mighty achievement. But I hope I have said enough to show that Italian thought and invention lent a well-defined sustenance to his unmatchable genius.

Shakespeare's indebtedness to Italy has many parallels in the history of English poetry. Chaucer, Shakespeare's greatest poetic predecessor, was an admiring disciple of the work of both Dante and Boccaccio. Milton, Shakespeare's successor on the throne of English poetry, was an appreciative and a grateful student in many Italian poetic schools. When we leap a century and face the great revival, of which Byron and Shelley were two exponents, we meet in English poetry with a passionate devotion to Italy, which was accentuated by Italy's contemporary suffering and oppression. The Brownings bore on high the same torch until it reached the hand of Swinburne, who was stirred by Italy's past and present fortune to his noblest poetic utterances. Swinburne was profoundly sympathetic with Italy in her manful struggles for liberty and unity, and he greeted exultingly her restoration to a place among the great nations. He saw in the colours of her flag, green and white and red, symbols of hope and light and life. Had he lived to be with us to-day we may say with confidence that he would have applied to Italy at this moment his own words of earlier date ·

> She feels her ancient breath and the old blood
> Move in her immortal veins.

Swinburne's poems on Italy worthily pursue a great tradition of English poetry. The Italian allegiance of Shakespeare, emperor of English poets, gives that tradition its most dazzling glory.

THE BRITISH ACADEMY

ANNUAL SHAKESPEARE LECTURES

I.
'WHAT TO EXPECT OF SHAKESPEARE'
By J. J. JUSSERAND
1911

II.
'CORIOLANUS'
By A. C. BRADLEY
1912

III.
'SHAKESPEARE AND GERMANY'
By ALOIS BRANDL
1913

IV.
'HAMLET AND ORESTES: A STUDY IN TRADITIONAL TYPES'
By GILBERT MURRAY
1914

Price Twenty-five Cents

New York
Oxford University Press American Branch
35 West 32nd Street
London: Humphrey Milford

CPSIA information can be obtained at www.ICGtesting.com
Printed in the USA
LVOW06s0407120915

453927LV00026B/698/P

9 781330 960370